BEOWULF
Meets His Match

Written by Julia Golding

Illustrated by Victor Rivas Villa

Published by Pearson Education Limited, Edinburgh Gate, Harlow, Essex, CM20 2JE
Registered company number: 872828

www.pearsonschools.co.uk

Text © Julia Golding 2012

Designed by Bigtop
Original illustrations © Pearson Education Limited 2012
Illustrated by Victor Rivas Villa

The right of Julia Golding to be identified as author of this work has been asserted by her in
accordance with the Copyright, Designs and Patents Act 1988.

First published 2012

21
10

British Library Cataloguing in Publication Data
A catalogue record for this book is available from the British Library

ISBN 978 0 435 07597 2

Printed and bound in Great Britain

Acknowledgements
We would like to thank the children and teachers of Bangor Central Integrated Primary School,
NI; Bishop Henderson C of E Primary School, Somerset; Brookside Community Primary
School, Somerset; Cheddington Combined School, Buckinghamshire; Cofton Primary School,
Birmingham; Dair House Independent School, Buckinghamshire; Deal Parochial School, Kent;
Holy Trinity Catholic Primary School, Chipping Norton; Lawthorn Primary School, North
Ayrshire; Newbold Riverside Primary School, Rugby and Windmill Primary School, Oxford for
their invaluable help in the development and trialling of the Bug Club resources.

Every effort has been made to contact copyright holders of material reproduced in this book.
Any omissions will be rectified in subsequent printings if notice is given to the publisher.

Contents

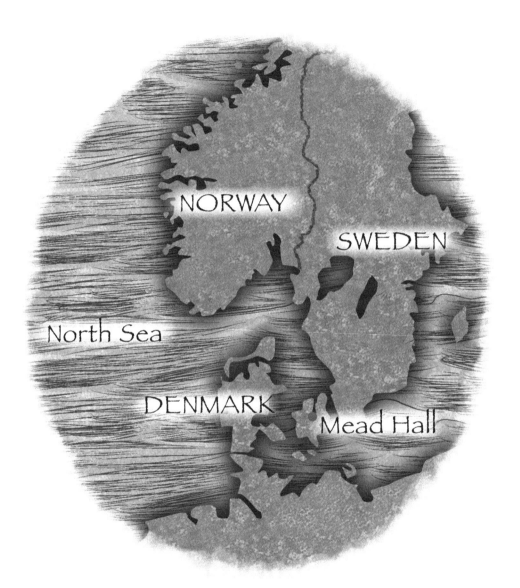

Who was Beowulf?

At some time between the middle of the 8th century and the beginning of the 11th (that means a very, very long time ago), an **Anglo-Saxon** poet wrote down 3000 lines of poetry about a hero called **Beowulf**. It was the superhero tale of its day. Beowulf is the brilliant and brave warrior who goes out in his special uniform of shining armour to fight super-villains; first the monster Grendel, then Grendel's mother and finally, at the end of his life, a dragon (but the dragon is another story!).

The story is set in Denmark not Britain, but maybe the Anglo-Saxons liked hearing about the troubles suffered by their **Viking** neighbours and enemies! We are lucky to have any record of the story at all, as only one copy survived the Middle Ages and that was almost burned in the 18th century.

There are plenty of retellings of the story but there has not been one quite like this. Let's hear from Grendel's mother for once and find out what she has to say for herself …

Chapter One
Even Monsters Have Mothers

You must have heard of my son, Grendel. He is the most famous, big, green bug-eyed monster in Denmark. For many years, he has been the most feared creature in the world. I am so proud of him. My shelf is full of the prizes he has won. Let me show you. Sorry they are a little battered. Look at that one with the six arms sticking out of the top. That is from the Ugliest Baby Monster Contest – he was awarded that in his first year.

Here is his portrait.

Aw, wasn't he sweet! That third eye of his is beautifully revolting. All the other mothers were so jealous of me, I can tell you. None of their babies was half so ugly.

The other trophies followed when he was full-grown:

Scariest Growl Competition (seven times champion!)

Sharpest Claws in **Scandinavia**

Smelliest Breath in Europe

Tidiest Garden in Denmark

Oops! I didn't mean to include that last one. To tell you the truth, I find that cup more than a little embarrassing. Who ever heard of a monster who liked gardening? I always worried when I saw Grendel digging his talons in the earth to plant marigolds, and using his teeth to prune his roses. However, my son insists it is his favourite award and won't let me get rid of it. I just keep it at the back where no one can see it.

From the day he learned to walk, I brought Grendel up to darken the dreams of men, as any responsible monster mother would. My son has been doing a good job, particularly since the **Danes** arrived to disturb our marsh. They make a lot of fuss about his visits. What do they expect if they move in on monster territory?

They built their hall right on *our* doorstep and have left so much litter, you would not believe it. There are piles of chicken bones, oyster shells and broken pots so that now the place stinks of humans rather than the lovely pong of swamp water. Part of me is pleased they came, because Grendel has finally had a chance to fulfil his early promise of being utterly nasty.

It wasn't always like this. Oh, dearie me, no. There was a time when Grendel first started school with the other monster children when he showed signs of going off track. I got worrying reports from his teachers that he was *nice* and *polite* to them. Aargh! That gave me a few grey hairs sprouting from my nostrils, I can tell you. Worse was to come. Grendel was seen in the corner of the playground making daisy chains, stroking the school kitten, and being picked on by the other monster kids.

Well, that had to stop AT ONCE. First step was to sort out the bullies. No mother will put up with her baby being hurt, even if he should have scared the bullies off himself. I marched into school and issued a few blood-curdling threats, breathed fire, pulled noses and stamped on claws.

That showed them!

I then tossed the daisy chains into the fire and told Grendel sharply that he was there to learn how to be a good monster. He was not to waste his time being nice (there is no worse insult to a monster). He is not stupid, my boy. After a bit of soul-searching, he changed his behaviour overnight.

The next day, I received a delighted message from his teacher that Grendel had produced a gruesome growl that morning at assembly that had shattered all the windows.

He had topped this performance by smelly burping at lunchtime, forcing all the other monster children to rush out for fresh air.

He was back on track for monster greatness.

He left school with an A* in Monster Studies. Do you want to see his certificate?

No?

What do you mean, 'No'?

You don't have time.

What do you mean, you 'don't have time'? That's strange, because I find I have time for a snack ...

Oh, so now you're sorry and would love to see it. Humph!

Now, where was I?

Ah yes, Grendel and the Danes.

Chapter Two
Beowulf the Bully

I thought we had come to an understanding with the Danes. We would scare them each night and eat a few from time to time to keep up our healthy diet of five limbs a day. In exchange, we would turn a blind eye to the fact that they were still on our home territory. But, typical humans, they did not keep to this agreement.

No, they called in the biggest bully of them all: Beowulf.

Being a good, responsible monster, my son tried to frighten Beowulf away but in return he got set upon by Beowulf's gang. Grendel barely escaped with his life. Thankfully, he was able to limp home to me. After hearing his sorry tale, I put bandages on his wounds and tucked him up in his old bed. I then gave him a soothing drink of hot swamp mud, bubbling with sulphur gas. He was asleep before he had drained the cup.

I sat beside his bed, smoothing the lank hair off his bruised face and bulbous nose. I remembered how he had looked that day long ago in the playground. I had faced down the bullies then, and I would do so again. Beowulf was going to regret he had ever laid a finger on *my* son.

I waited until nightfall. The Danes kept to their usual behaviour and were having yet another of their awful parties. The noise was so loud that the trophies on my shelf were jumping. I could even hear snatches of the songs. They were singing about killing my son. They thought he was dead. Hah! It takes more than a little tussle with humans to kill Grendel.

At midnight, the feast finally came to an end and I could hear the party-goers shouting loud 'good nights' to each other. Oh yes, it was going to be a permanent 'good night' for some of them if I had my way.

I took out my hair curlers and put red varnish on my talons as I prepared for my little visit to the neighbours. I checked my reflection in the mirror. I looked truly ghastly. One glance at my ugly face would be enough to make any normal man faint with terror.

Perfect: that was exactly the impression I wanted to make. I may be pushing a hundred and fifty in monster years, but I can still scare the humans as well as any girl monster of my species.

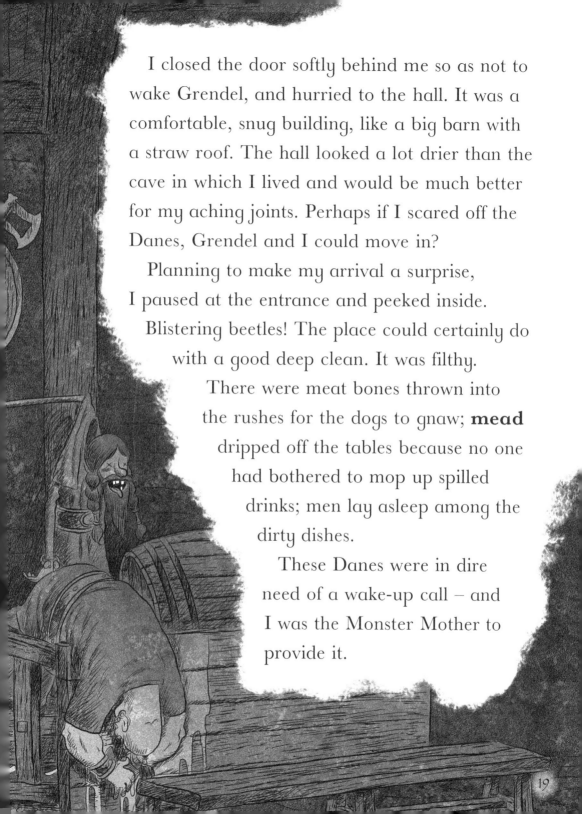

I closed the door softly behind me so as not to wake Grendel, and hurried to the hall. It was a comfortable, snug building, like a big barn with a straw roof. The hall looked a lot drier than the cave in which I lived and would be much better for my aching joints. Perhaps if I scared off the Danes, Grendel and I could move in?

Planning to make my arrival a surprise, I paused at the entrance and peeked inside.

Blistering beetles! The place could certainly do with a good deep clean. It was filthy.

There were meat bones thrown into the rushes for the dogs to gnaw; **mead** dripped off the tables because no one had bothered to mop up spilled drinks; men lay asleep among the dirty dishes.

These Danes were in dire need of a wake-up call – and I was the Monster Mother to provide it.

"Aargh!" I burst into the hall.

I shook my head so my wild black locks flew about my face like snakes. "You should be ashamed of yourselves!" Spit foamed from my blood-red lips. "I bet your mothers don't know you live like pigs in a sty!" I threw a helmet topped with a boar's tusk across the room. It hit a startled warrior. He fell over like a skittle.

By now all the other men had begun to wake up. Screams broke out.

"I thought we had killed Grendel!" gasped one chubby fighter. He grappled for his sword.

"That's not Grendel," shouted another. "That's his mum!"

"And you know what they say," yelled a third. "The female of the species is more deadly than the male!"

The yelling hit new heights. Good: so they *had* heard of me.

I swooped on a red-haired warrior and picked him up in my claws. "You are old enough to know better than to live in such a mess. Have you no shame?" I asked.

"W-what?" spluttered my captive.

"Are you Beowulf?" I squeezed him in the middle.

"No!" he gasped.

A tall man leaped out in front of me, white teeth gleaming in a smug handsome face. "I am Beowulf! Unhand that man, foul creature!"

So here was the bully boy. I dropped my captive, not interested in the followers when the main target was in sight.

"You call me foul?" I screeched. "My standards of personal hygiene are much higher than yours, stinky boy."

Beowulf looked surprised by this line of attack. He took a quick sniff af his shirt. "I do not smell."

"Yes, you do. Your pals might be too polite to tell you, but when was the last time you had a proper wash?"

Beowulf frowned.

"And I mean behind your ears *and* the back of your neck, too?" I folded my arms.

He blushed. "What has that got to do with anything?"

"Hmm, I thought so. You bullies are all the same. You are just spoiled little boys at heart."

Beowulf really didn't like that insult. He drew his sword. I could have beaten him easily if he had fought on his own, but all his men took out their weapons and waved them at me. Seeing I was outnumbered, I settled for stomping on the tables, ripping the tapestries from the walls and setting fire to the place before running for cover.

"I'll be back!" I shouted as I raced for the marsh.

"Don't bother – I'll come to you!" replied Beowulf.

Good. I really must have annoyed him with my comments if he was upset enough to suggest a rematch on my home ground.

Chapter Three
The Battle of the Lake

Now the reason I was pleased to have Beowulf threatening me with a home match was that my cave is really tricky to find and dangerous to enter.

First, you have to push your way through prickly bushes to reach the shore of the lake. The surface looks like a polished black gem stone, so dark and forbidding that taking a swim would be the last thing on any human's mind. In winter, tree roots dip their frozen limbs into the water. Ice forms like a lace collar around the lake's edge.

Added to this, I have my own pack of water beasts to scare off unwanted callers. No one but a monster can be happy in such a place.

The real secret to my fortress lies in the depths. I found the cave quite by accident when fishing for eels. The entrance is underwater. You have to swim through a tunnel before coming up into my parlour. And that's where I'll be waiting with my collection of sharp chopping knives. At dinner time.

I did not expect Beowulf to get that far. My water beasts are well trained. A loyal pack of lizard creatures, they guard my door. They have teeth like sharks, scales like dragons and webbed feet, so they usually stop an invader in his tracks.

Just in case this Beowulf was better than most, I decided to hide Grendel. I moved him to the inner chamber and made a straw monster to take his place, complete with a wooden dragon head that I had hacked off a Viking ship last winter. (The sailors had moored on my beach without paying the parking fee so naturally I'd chased them off and taken their boat as a prize.)

It was as well I took these steps to defend my home because I heard the water beasts yelping in alarm. The invader was here! Then they began to howl. Beowulf had pulled one of them on to the shore and killed him! Not my darling little water beasts! How could anyone be so cruel to my puppies?

"Right, that does it, Beowulf! Show yourself in my cave and you will regret it!" I howled.

"What's the matter, Mum?" Grendel called feebly from the inner chamber.

"Never you mind, Grendelkins. Let Mummy deal with this horrid little human," I replied.

A splashing in the water-entrance alerted me to Beowulf's approach.

"Keep out of sight!" I warned Grendel. I didn't want him to fight while he was still feeling poorly.

"All right, Mum. Whatever you think is best," he said.

I had no time to reply because an arm, clad in chain-mail, thrust itself out of the waterhole. I sank my teeth in.

Ow! That man had a good **armourer**. I felt one of my teeth crack. I still managed to keep hold, and dragged the human hero onto the earth floor. He was wet and slippery like a water rat.

"Don't you know it is rude to burst in without an invitation?" I growled.

"Pond-Hag, your days are numbered!" shouted Beowulf, hitting me on the bridge of my nose with his sword. The blade bounced off. I have a lovely bumpy, warty patch on my face that turns away any weapon. Beowulf looked surprised that his blade had failed.

Hah! You underestimated this monster lady, Beowulf.

Seizing my chance, I picked Beowulf up and threw him across the room. He hit my shelf of trophies and slid down to sit on the Monster Baby Cup. That must have hurt.

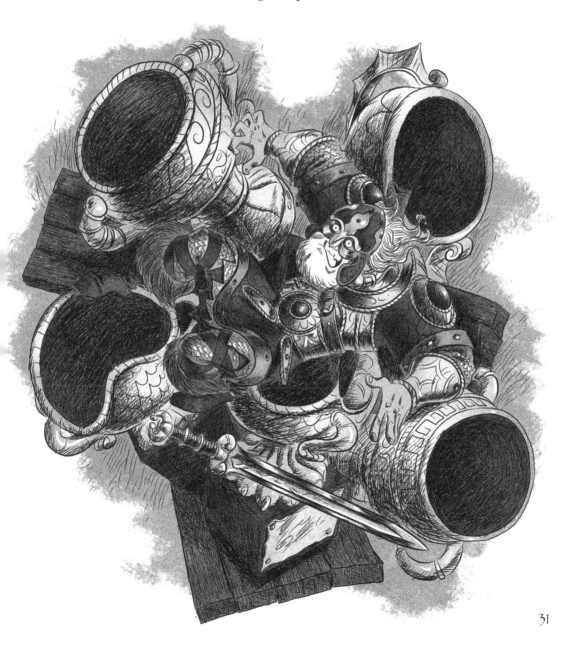

"You think you can hurt my son and get away with it!" I said. "Well, think again, Beo-Bully!"

"*Hurt* your son? I gave him a mortal wound earlier, Pond-Hag. I see he crawled home and now lies dead on his bed there, and good riddance!" Beowulf replied as he got back to his feet.

Of course I knew he hadn't really killed Grendel – only injured him in the fight in the king's hall. Beowulf was fooled by the straw dummy, as I intended. But still, he had hurt my little boy. Rage got the better of me; I charged the warrior and shook him until his helmet flew off. I then gave him a taste of the hag-hug. Heard of a bear-hug? Well, a hag-hug is similar but ten times more powerful. Beowulf gasped and spluttered.

"Not such a big man now, are you? Not on your own, on my home ground," I taunted him.

Beowulf flailed around, his blows bouncing off my hard skull and bony neck. Then he blindly poked his sword hilt up my nostril ...

Major ouch! I had to let go. This was the one weak point on my face and Beowulf was lucky enough to find it by accident. My eyes were watering so hard I could barely see where I was going. I crashed into the pots and pans by the hearth.

34

"My friend, the Danish king, has promised me much gold for killing you. It will be my pleasure," Beowulf cried. He leaped the low table and grabbed one of my kitchen knives from the counter.

"Don't you go getting my knives dirty!" I yelled. "And don't track muddy footprints over my clean floors!"

Then, disaster! As I rushed to stop him, I tripped over the helmet he had carelessly left on the floor, fell, and hit my head on my stone fireplace.

Oh, blistering beetles, I was done for.

Chapter Four
Things Change

When I woke up, I found Grendel leaning over me,
placing a cold flannel on the big bump on my forehead.
I have lots of bumps on my head but this was a new one.

"Mum, Mum, are you all right?"

I opened an eye. Then a second, then the third.
"What happened?"

Grendel sighed with relief, green smoke curling from
his mouth. "That bully made a bit of a mess, I'm
afraid, Mum."

I sat up. My lovely little cave was trashed. All my cooking pots dented, my knives taken, my collection of trophies stamped into the dirt.

"I'll kill him!" I wailed.

Grendel patted my shoulder. "No, no, leave it, Mum. He's not worth it. He thinks we're dead, anyway."

He pointed to the remains of the fake Grendel I had made. Beowulf had carried off the wooden dragon's head. Idiot. Humans are so easy to trick. He must have been so scared that I would revive that he didn't take time to look properly at what he had grabbed as his prize.

"But he broke my trophies!" I cried.

Grendel gave me a sheepish grin. "Not all of them," he said. "I managed to hide one from him." And he pulled out from behind his back the cup for the Tidiest Garden in Denmark.

I started wailing even louder.

"And I can mend the others," Grendel said quickly. "You know I'm good with my hands. I've been thinking: it seems clear to me that no amount of scaring is going to get rid of these Danes. And they are ruining the peace and quiet with their loud parties. Why don't we move?"

My jaw dropped open, releasing a puff of smoke. "Us? Leave Denmark? But it has always been our home!"

"Yes, but things change and we need to change with them," argued Grendel.

He had a point. As much as I wanted revenge, I did not like the idea of going up against Bully Beowulf for another fight. He now knew where my weak spot was.

"Where could we go, Grendel?" I asked.

Grendel cleared his throat.

"You know I exchange cuttings and seeds with my gardening pals?"

I nodded. I had never approved but had vowed not to interfere with his hobby as it brought him so much innocent pleasure.

"One of them told me of a nice little opening in Loch Ness. It appears that they have a vacancy for a water monster or two."

"Loch Ness?" I asked. "Where's that?"

"Scotland, about a week's swim from here."

Grendel looked pleased that I had not rejected the idea immediately.

"He says that it is lovely gardening country with soft mists to hide in, rolling green mountains to climb and lots of deer for eating."

I licked my lips. You can enjoy eels for only so many decades.

"I like venison. But what about the water beasts?"
I asked, already half persuaded.

"Oh, they can come too. It's a big loch with plenty of
room for your pets."

I rubbed my hands and looked around the cavern of
which I had once been so proud. I would never feel the
same way about it now that Beowulf had broken in.
I wouldn't be able to sleep quietly at night
knowing he might be back.

"Let's give Loch Ness a chance then," I said. "Leave these Danes to their marsh. They can have it. I hope they rot here." I wrinkled my nose. "But what of these Scottish people? Are they quiet and well behaved? No loud parties? They play soft, tuneful musical instruments?"

"Oh yes," said Grendel, too quickly. (I suspect now that he was crossing his talons behind his back!) "They are as quiet as mice."

I didn't quite trust his answer even then, but anything had to be better than years of rowdy Danes as our neighbours.

So Grendel and I packed up that very night and swam all the way to Scotland. He brought his favourite plants, and I my trophies.

So now you've seen my new home, why don't you stay to dinner?

No?

You've made other plans?

Little human, why are you running? Come back!

Drat.

"Grendel, Grendel! It will be fish for supper again, I'm afraid. Finish scaring off the next bus-load of humans and I'll have it ready on the table for you."

Loch Ness has turned out to be a very good home to a monster and his mother. Perhaps you will come and visit us again one day?

Glossary and Pronunciation Guide

Anglo-Saxons   name given to the people who lived in England until the Norman Conquest in 1066

armourer   someone who makes or repairs armour and weapons

Beowulf   say 'Bay-o-wolf'

Danes   people who come from Denmark

mead   strong drink made from honey and water

Scandinavia   the countries Norway, Sweden and Denmark

Vikings   Scandinavian 'pirates' who raided the coasts of Northern and Western Europe from the 8th to the 11th centuries